FIVE LITTLE
FOXES OF
FAITH

FIVE LITTLE FOXES OF FAITH

by Frederick K.C. Price

FAITH ONE
PUBLISHING

Unless otherwise indicated, all scripture quotations are taken from *The New King James Version*. Copyright 1979, 1980, 1982, Thomas Nelson, Inc., Publishers. Used by permission.

6th Printing
Five Little Foxes of Faith

ISBN 10: 1883798191
ISBN 13: 9781883798192

Catch us the foxes,
The little foxes that spoil the vines,
For our vines have tender grapes.

(Song of Solomon 2:15, NKJV)

Contents

Introduction

OVER THE YEARS, the Lord has led me to teach on many areas of faith—or, more aptly, the faith lifestyle. The Bible tells us in Habakkuk 2:4 and Romans 1:17 that *the just shall live by faith.* Living by faith is not merely a suggestion, but a commandment of God. That means we are supposed to live by faith every day of our lives.

We are further told this in Hebrews 11:6: *But without faith it is impossible to please Him.* In other words, if we do not use our faith and base our lifestyle on it, there is no way we can please our heavenly Father. That is clearly what the Bible says.

We can read and study the Bible every day, mark passages with colored pens and pencils, quote scripture forward and backward, go to church every Sunday and to Bible study every week, and still miss it when it comes to living by faith. In fact, it is so easy to miss God that many people never realize they are doing it.

One reason it is so easy to miss Him is that we aren't aware of the smaller conflicts. The Bible calls these hindrances *the little foxes that spoil the vines* (Song of Solomon 2:15). We may take every effort to not let major spiritual issues trip us up, but usually it is the "little foxes" that cause us to stumble. What we as believers need to realize is that those overlooked faults can nullify our faith as easily as the larger issues. That makes them equally dangerous.

In this book, we will look at some of these hindrances to our spiritual growth—not "the little white lie" we may have told at home or at the office, or any of the other mess-ups that are obvious sins. Instead, we will discuss some hidden sins that we may not have recognized that can keep our faith from functioning at its fullest. Many may have committed some of these faults over so long a period of time that they may no longer be conscious of doing them, let alone know they are deviating from God's Word.

This is why we are told in Second Timothy 2:15 to *Be diligent to present yourself approved to God, a worker who does not need to be ashamed, rightly dividing the word of truth.* If we are diligent students, we will learn that none of what the enemy sends our way can trip us up. And more importantly, we will not trip ourselves up with any of the "little foxes" that keep us from achieving God's best in our lives.

1

Unforgiveness
A Snare to Our Faith

E VEN THOSE WHO may not have been Christians for long may know someone who has said, "I can never forgive her [or him] for what she [or he] did." That person may be wonderful and loving in many other areas, but if someone so much as mentions the victim of their unforgiveness he or she gets mean and ugly very quickly. That grudge is something they seem to desire to carry around forever. The real tragedy is that as long as the individual holds the grudge, God cannot forgive him or her, or answer their prayers.

In case you are thinking, "That can't be true. God always forgives us whenever we ask Him to," notice what Jesus says about unforgiveness in Mark 11:22-26:

> *So Jesus answered and said to them, "Have faith in God. "For assuredly, I say to you, whoever says to this mountain, 'Be removed and be cast in the sea,' and does not doubt in his heart, but*

believes that those things he says will be done, he will have whatever he says.

'Therefore I say to you, whatever things you ask when you pray, believe that you receive them, and you, will have them.

"And whenever you stand praying, if you have anything against anyone, forgive him, that your Father in heaven may also forgive you your trespasses.

"But if you do not forgive, neither will your Father in heaven forgive your trespasses."

Unforgiveness has been a stumbling block for many Christians, preventing them from receiving the Father's best in their lives. And the fact that it has not been talked about in the context of the faith message has been a grave mistake. Sometimes, without realizing it, unforgiveness can be lodged in the heart, and it will stop faith every time. It is like pulling the plug on a lamp that is being used to give light in a room.

Another scripture that gives us God's view on unforgiveness is Matthew 6:9-15:

"In this manner, therefore pray:
 Our Father in heaven,
 Hallowed be Your name.
 Your kingdom come.
 Your will be done
 On earth as it is in heaven.

Give us this day our daily bread.
And forgive us our debts,
As we forgive our debtors.
And do not lead us into temptation,
But deliver us from the evil one.
For Yours is the kingdom and the power
and the glory forever Amen.

"For if you forgive men their trespasses, your
heavenly Father will also forgive you. "But if you
do not forgive men their trespasses, neither will
your Father forgive your trespasses."

We control the Father's ability to forgive us by how we forgive. We can be living right from the standpoint of morality. We can be praying, studying the Word, tithing, and making the right confessions. But if we harbor anything against anyone, God cannot forgive us, because that is the way He has designed the system.

Jesus says in Luke 6:37, *"Judge not, and you shall not be judged. Condemn not, and you shall not be condemned. Forgive, and you will be forgiven."* Turn that around, and the outlook becomes very grim: judge, and you shall be judged. Condemn, and you shall be condemned. Forgive not, and you will not be forgiven.

Unforgiveness is something we don't have the luxury of entertaining, especially with the enemy prowling like a roaring lion, seeking whom he may devour. Yet entertaining unforgiveness is a temptation to which many people succumb. They savor a grudge as though it were a gourmet meal, turning each bite over on their tongues, and letting it dance across every one of their taste buds to get its full flavor.

While these unforgivers are doing that, they are literally poisoning themselves, spiritually speaking.

That is why God tells us in Ephesians 4:32, *And be kind to one another, tenderhearted, forgiving one another, even as God in Christ forgave you.*

And in Colossians 3:13 it says, *bearing with one another, and forgiving one another, if anyone has a complaint against another; even as Christ forgave you, so you also must do.*

God doesn't want us to fall into the trap of not forgiving someone—and a trap is exactly what unforgiveness is. If you don't forgive, the heavenly Father cannot hear you; therefore, your confession of faith will not get through to Him. One cannot even say he or she forgot to forgive someone. The reason they can't is because it's really not about forgiving a person. It could be that they have made unforgiveness such a habit that it is automatic, and they don't even think about it.

Think back to when you first learned to drive. You may have had to keep looking down for the brake or accelerator pedal to be sure you knew where to put your foot. But after a while you became so familiar with the car that you didn't have to think about where the pedals were. When you drove into traffic, you could stop, slow down, or accelerate by instinct.

Learning *not* to forgive occurs in the same way. What you need to do to correct unforgiveness is to learn to forgive people without even thinking about what you are doing. It may take some effort in the beginning, but the more you do it, the easier it will become.

The question then becomes how far should we take forgiveness. How often should we forgive, and how far out of the way should a person go to forgive? After all, we don't want to risk becoming fanatical about the matter. A comparable situation would be when people claim that if you read the Bible too much it will affect your mind. You had better believe reading the Bible will affect your mind. It will renew it!

Concerning the issue of how often God expects us to forgive, Peter asked Jesus about this subject in Matthew 18:21-22:

> *Then Peter came to Him and said, "Lord, how often shall my brother sin against me, and I forgive him? Up to seven times?"*

Peter really thought he was being generous by saying, "Up to seven times?" But notice how Jesus answers the question in the next verse:

> *Jesus said to him, "I do not say to you, up to seven times, but up to seventy times seven."*

Seventy time seven works out to be 490 times. If you live to be 50 or 60 years old or so, you could forgive the same person two or three times a year. That doesn't sound like an unreasonable amount of time or effort.

But is that what Jesus is really saying here? Let's consider another passage of scripture that puts more light on the subject. Luke 17:3-4 refers to the same incident as discussed in Matthew 18:21-22, but with a bit more amplification. In fact, it amplifies the story so much that I suggest you prepare yourself for the shock.

> *"Take heed to yourselves. If your brother sins against you, rebuke him; and if he repents, forgive him.*
>
> *"And if he sins against you seven times in a day, and seven times in a day he returns to you, saying, 'I repent,' you shall forgive him."*

Put what we read in Matthew and Luke together. In Matthew, Peter asked Jesus if he should forgive someone who sins against him seven times. Jesus told him that He did not say forgive the man seven times, but seventy times seven. In Luke, Jesus says:

"And if he sins against you seven times in a day." If we put the seven times a day with seventy times seven, it adds up to 490 times a day. Not 490 times in a lifetime, but 490 times in a day.

If we sit down and do the math with these figures,

you will find that 490 times a day equals out to 3,430 times a week. Multiply that figure by 52 weeks and the total is 178,360 times a year. That's a lot of forgiving.

Why would the Lord require us to be that extravagant? Because of one very important biblical precept: our heavenly Father never asks us to do what He is not willing to do Himself.

This verse of scripture shows us how much God is willing to forgive us. He is willing to forgive us 178,360 times a year. That makes up a lot of mercy that is being extended toward us. How can we dare forgive one another any less than that?

Not only that, but you can see how vitally important unforgiveness is to the Father by how much the Word has to say about the subject. We even have numbers on it, numbers we can figure out; numbers we can work with. The Lord went to an extraordinary degree of effort to make His point, and to make sure we could not misinterpret it.

The Unforgiving Servant

Another place where God lavished effort to make His point is Matthew 18:23-35. In those verses of scripture, we have a parable that illustrates these points: the mercy of God, the liability of unforgiveness, and how far some must go to come into agreement with God's way of thinking.

"Therefore the kingdom of heaven is like a certain king who wanted to settle accounts with his servants.

"And when he had begun to settle accounts, one was brought to him who owed him ten thousand talents.

"But as he was not able to pay, his master commanded that he be sold, with his wife and children and all that he had, and that payment be made.

"The servant therefore fell down before him, saying, 'Master, have patience with me, and I will pay you all.'

"Then the master of that servant was moved with compassion, released him, and forgave him the debt.

"But that servant went out and found one of his fellow servants who owed him a hundred denarii; and he laid hands on him and took him by the throat, saying, 'Pay me what you owe!'

"So his fellow servant fell down at his feet and begged him, saying, 'Have patience with me, and I will pay you all.'

"And he would not, but went and threw him into prison till he should pay the debt.

"So when his fellow servants saw what had been done, they were very grieved, and came and told their master all that had been done.

"Then his master, after he had called him,

said to him, 'You wicked servant! I forgave you all that debt because you begged me.

'Should you not also have had compassion on your fellow servant, just as I had pity on you?'

"And his master was angry, and delivered him to the torturers until he should pay all that was due to him.

"So My heavenly Father also will do to you if each of you, from his heart, does not forgive his brother his trespasses."

The Roman term *denarii* and the Greco-Roman term *talents* are not words for currency that were used in our English language as they were used in biblical times, so the story still may not have the impact on you that it should. But you'll get the idea.

When the *denarii* and *talents* are reduced to dollars and cents, one can more fully appreciate the magnitude of the amounts involved in this teaching by Jesus. While working on this book in 1993, ten thousand talents of silver in the U.S. economy was worth approximately ten million dollars. Ten thousand talents of gold was worth approximately nineteen and three-quarters of a million dollars or $19,750,000.

At that same time, one denarii was worth roughly twenty cents, so one hundred denarii was about twenty dollars.

The average person doesn't know anyone who would forgive them of a $19,750,000 debt. In fact, if someone owed their creditors that much, and could not pay, the creditors would probably do better by taking them apart and selling them molecule by molecule to get at least some of their money back. But the lord of the servant did not do that.

Instead, he forgave the servant.

That show of compassion did not transfer through that servant to the other servant. He was so hardhearted that despite the goodness that had been shown him, he would not turn and express that same capacity to forgive a fellow servant who owed him a much smaller debt. His hardheartedness is not only amazing, but it constituted a slap in the face of the master who had forgiven him.

We previously cited Ephesians 4:32, but I want to point out something in that verse that ties directly into what I pointed out in Matthew:

> *And be kind to one another, tenderhearted, forgiving one another, even as God in Christ forgave you.*

What Paul is referring to here is this: When we accept Christ as our personal Savior and Lord, and move out of spiritual death into spiritual life, God remits our sin. He wipes spiritual death out, just as one would erase something from a white board. Then, He treats it as though it never existed. This is what Paul means when he writes…even as God in Christ forgave you. Sin is like a $19,750,000 debt that has already been forgiven.

When God asks us to forgive one another, He considers that the same as our pardoning one another of a $20 debt. Considering the great amount God has forgiven us, and what we get out of it, the amount He requires us to forgive one another, pales and shrinks in comparison.

Even if you think, "You just don't know what that person did to me." Well, God knows. No, certainly you shouldn't go back and let that individual beat your brains out, but forgive him, and don't let anything someone does to you affect your relationship with the heavenly Father. If I got into someone's yard, and the person's dog came up and bit me, I don't hold it against the dog. I forgive the dog for being a dog. However, I also make it a point not to go back into that yard again and subject myself to the dog's attack.

When you forgive someone, you are not condoning their actions. You're simply not letting what that person did sour your attitude and affect your relationship with the heavenly Father.

Do What Jesus Did

"What should I do, then?" you might ask. Do what the Bible says. The Lord says in Romans 12:19 that *"Vengeance is Mine, I will repay."* Turn what happened to you over to the Lord. If God is not big enough to handle it, what makes you think you are?

Consider what happened to Jesus. They drove nails into His hands, put a crown of thorns on His head, and humiliated Him. But all Jesus did was ask God to forgive them because they did not know what they were doing. If you are part of the Body of Christ, or what I call ambassadors for Christ in the earth realm, how can you possibly hold a grudge against anyone, knowing what the Bible says?

Paul reminds us in Hebrews 4:15, *For we do not have a High Priest who cannot sympathize with our weaknesses, but was in all points tempted as we are, yet without sin.* If anyone knows how much you hurt because of what someone did to you, it is Jesus.

He knows exactly what you are going through. What He's doing—through His Word and His example—is showing you how to stop hurting, and how to prevent yourself from being hurt again.

One thing I have developed, and I thank God for it, is that I don't hold anything in my heart against anyone. There have been many situations in my life in which it was very tempting to hold something against someone. Those situations continue to come up, even today, but I don't let them bother me. I shake off what happens like water off a duck's back, and let it go.

Forgiving is one virtue we should all develop. God knows your heart, and He knows the cruelty of whatever happened. We can rest assured that He understands and is ready to handle any situation on our behalf. All we need to do is allow Him to do it. That is why He tells us in First Peter 5:7, *casting all your care upon Him, for He cares for you.* He wants you to let Him handle it.

Don't allow yourself to be mistreated by anyone. I don't believe God wants us to do that, but don't hold it against that person for the mistreatment you have received. If you are a woman, don't let your bad experiences with the opposite sex sour you, or get you to say, "There are no good men."

There are many good people

Sometimes we say things glibly, without thinking about what we are saying. There are certainly no-good men, along with no-good husbands, no-good women, no-good wives, no-good kids, and no-good parents. But all are not that way. Instead of saying there are no good men, say: "There are some good men out there, and I believe one of them is mine, in Jesus' name."

Making that kind of confession will help you get out of a mode of unforgiveness. It will build up faith within you for meeting *that* good man or that good woman. Romans 10:17 says, *So then faith comes by hearing, and hearing by the word of God.* It will also start your faith working on the situation and allow God to bring the right man [or woman] to you that much sooner.

Some people will not forgive others for their skin

color, as though that person had a choice about whether he would be born black, white or brown. It is not that person's fault for being his color any more than it is anyone else's fault for being another color. We have no right to be prejudiced against anyone because of his or her race.

Paul says in Acts 17:26 that God *has made from one blood every nation of men to dwell on all the face of the earth.* When you hold something against others because of their color, you are holding something against the Father God, because He is the one who made everyone. God made them, so they must be alright with Him.

Some may say, "Yeah, but it was those black people who bombed out our cities. It was the black people who burned down the building."

You are mistaken. By far, the overwhelming number of black people have never burned down anything. It may have been a black *person* who burned something down, but it wasn't every black person or anything close to that.

There is a principle we're dealing with here. I will forgive people for anything they do because that is what my heavenly Father tells me to do. If people lie on me, that's their problem. My Father is well able to handle the situation as long as I keep my heart clean, and my spirit open.

I wish everyone would say, "Fred Price is a great fellow." But I'm not going to lose any sleep if they don't.

Most of all, we need to learn to forgive ourselves. For some, this has been an especially big stumbling block. Not forgiving yourself will cause you to miss out on the blessings God has in store for you. It will also leave open a door through which the devil can come in and haunt your mind, even months or years later. He will use that point of entry to keep you feeling guilty, dirty and unloved.

Under the Blood of Jesus

When you expect God to forgive you for something you did or said, what transpired is placed under the blood of Jesus. No matter what you did, God will not hold it against you. Further, He will never bring it to your mind. To Him, it is as though it never happened.

This is why we are told in First John 1:9, *If we confess our sins, He is faithful and just to forgive us our sins and to cleanse us from all unrighteousness.* Once we ask God to forgive us, that is the end of the matter, as far as our right standing with God is concerned. There may still be consequences for certain offenses we have to face in a natural way because we have set certain things in motion, but it has nothing to do with our relationship with God. He loves us, and He does not remember the past. He is a God of now, and He sees only the present.

You may not feel at first as if you are forgiven, but don't let that influence you. First John 1:9 doesn't say,

"If we confess our sins, He is faithful, and just to make us feel like we are forgiven." It says...*He is faithful and just to forgive us*.... God says that once you ask Him for forgiveness, it is immediately done, so don't let the enemy intimidate you through your emotions. Take what God says by faith, confess it, walk in it, because as Paul instructs in Second Corinthians 5:7...*we walk by faith, not by sight.*

Once you believe this fact and walk in it, the joy of the Lord will come. But never let your feeling be what determines your relationship with God. Always base where you are with God on His Word, and on your faith in that Word.

I pointed out earlier that we should be casting all our care upon Him. That is, upon God, because He cares for us. That is what we should do when we ask God to forgive us of a particular sin. We have to accept God's forgiveness by faith, and have the good taste not to bring the matter up or give it another thought—except to make sure we don't commit the sin again. Forgive yourself and move on with God in Jesus' name.

2

Worry
The Sin of Not Trusting God

ANOTHER LITTLE FOX that tries to eat away our faith and is just as important as unforgiveness and just as unrecognized, is the sin of worry. Notice, I call it the *sin* of worry. If most people were asked to make a list of sins, they would write down such obvious ones as lying, murder, fornication and adultery. Very few, if any, would have *worry* on their list, and yet worry is one of the worst sins any Christian can commit.

If you are walking [living] by faith, you should not worry or have fear of anything. That is because worry is unbelief. It is a lack of faith, and the Bible says that anything not of faith is sin. When we worry, we are telling God, "I cannot trust you to take care of this for me." Most of us would not dream of saying that to God, yet that is exactly what we do when we worry. It is a direct affront to the heavenly Father.

Most Christians consider worry a part of life. They consider it normal to worry about their husbands, their wives, their kids, their job, their finances, the future. In fact, they feel guilty when they are *not* concerned about those things. But if we are trusting God, what are we worrying about? The answer should be "nothing." That is why Paul says in Philippians 4:6:

> *Be anxious for nothing, but in everything by prayer and supplication, with thanksgiving, let your requests be made known to God.*

The word *anxious* literally means "anxious to the point of distraction," and, of course, the enemy wants us to be distracted. We can become so wrapped up in some concern that we don't take time to pray, to tell anyone about Jesus, or to even live right. That is when the enemy will come at us like a flood to wipe us out.

I say this: Don't allow your husband, your wife, or anyone or anything to become a distraction. Use faith in and on the situation. Make a request to God about it, stand in faith, and praise Him for the answer, because He tells us…*in everything by prayer and supplication, with thanksgiving, let your requests be made known to God.*

God wants to hear our requests, and He wants to do something about them for us. But for Him to do what He wants to do on our behalf, we have to apply our faith. Jesus tells us in Mark 11:23:

"For assuredly, I say to you, whoever says to this mountain, 'Be removed and be cast into the sea,' and does not doubt in his heart, but believes that those things he says will be done, he will have whatever he says."

In fact, Jesus states this in triplicate. For your faith to work, you must say what you want God to do for you. If you don't say it, it will not get done. It is as simple as that.

Giving God Your Cares

Another scripture that will help in applying faith to a given situation is First Peter 5:7: *casting all your care upon Him, for He cares for you.*

Many years ago, there was a song that advised, *"Take your burdens to the Lord and leave them there."* Too many people go to the Lord with a burden, then pick it up and carry it away with them. They listen to the Word of God, but they don't turn loose the things they are praying about. If they hold onto them, God doesn't have them, so He cannot answer those prayers.

You may think, as one lady did when she asked me this question: "Brother Price, I understand what you're saying. I know I need to cast my care on the Lord. But tell me how I am supposed to do that. How am I supposed to cast my husband on the Lord? He's six-foot-three and weighs 235 pounds. I can't even pick him up. How do I cast him on the Lord?"

Obviously, she could not cast her husband on the Lord literally, but here's what God showed me: Get a piece of paper, or more than one if needed, and write down every care on it. When you are finished, go to the waste paper basket with that paper, and say the following:

> "Lord, You told me to cast all my cares upon You, for You care for me. Here are all my cares, everything I'm concerned with, and in the name of Jesus, I cast them all upon You. Thank You, Lord, in Jesus' name."

After you say that, drop that paper in the waste paper basket and leave it there. If you leave it there, you no longer have it. That makes you free.

Free people don't stay up all night, wringing their hands and worrying. They sleep all night because their minds are clear, and they have no troubling thoughts because they know the Lord is "on the case." Or as Philippians 4:7 puts it:

> *and the peace of God, which surpasses all understanding, will guard your hearts and minds through Christ Jesus.*

Here is a good way to measure whether you have actually cast your care upon the Lord. If you don't have peace about it, that means you still have it.

The word *understanding* in Philippians 4:7 refers to

human understanding. We are told in Proverbs 3:5 to *Trust in the Lord with all your heart, and lean not on your own understanding.* As Christians we must trust the Lord with our hearts, or with our spirits, when it comes to the things of God. Our human understanding can't comprehend them, because they don't make sense. But sense is not faith, and we are supposed to walk by faith, not by sight, or by our senses.

When we try using our natural, human understanding, we're inclined to think, "How can I live without worrying about my wife? I can't do it!" That is why God says:... *and lean not on your own understanding.*

If the devil can get us to focus on our own understanding, instead of the Word of God, he will win every time. He wants us to use *our* understanding, but we should never give him that advantage. We must continue to stand on God's Word, and we will operate in the peace of God.

Until I found out how to operate in the peace of God, I felt as if I could not pay the bills without worrying about them. But the peace of God passes all understanding, and the good thing about it is that we don't have to understand it. All we have to do is enjoy it.

When we think about it, there is really very little we have to understand in order to enjoy the benefits. For instance, if someone drops a match into a jar of gasoline, the gasoline will explode and blow the jar apart. However, when we drive an automobile, we mix gasoline and fire in the engine, and the engine does not blow apart. Unless you are well versed in chemistry or auto mechanics, you don't understand why that doesn't happen, and nor do you care. You just want to take advantage of the car's power when you're driving.

Here is something else to consider. Paul says in Philippians 4:7 that *the peace of God... will guard your hearts and minds through Christ Jesus.* It is obvious that your heart is not your mind, because hearts and minds are mentioned as two separate things. If they were the same, Paul would have said either "shall keep your heart" or "shall keep your mind." He would not have said both *hearts and minds.*

As I have said before, the heart is the spirit. It is the real you. We are spirits, we have souls, and we live in physical bodies. Our minds are located in our souls.

If God's peace is in you, it will allow your heart and mind to exert an influence over your body and keep you in line with the Word. Many times, when a person's body is not functioning correctly, it is because he does not have peace in his heart and mind.

Think About These Things

If we are not supposed to worry, what are we supposed to think about? According to Philippians 4:8, we should concentrate on these things:

> *Finally, brethren, whatever things are true, whatever things are noble, whatever things are just,*

32

whatever things are pure, whatever things are lovely, whatever things are of good report, if there is any virtue and if there is anything praise-worthy–meditate on these things.

Things that are true, noble, just, pure, lovely, of good report, things that have virtue and things that are praise-worthy are the things we should think on, not on what calamities can befall our families or our jobs. Those things are not pure, lovely, or of good report. Instead, we should confess that the angels of the Lord are encamped around us and our family, that whatever we do shall prosper, including our job, and that nothing we do shall fail.

We should think about all the blessings God promises us in His Word. The more we confess them, the more faith we will have for them, and the more we operate in this principle the more what we say will come to pass.

To fully operate in this principle, it is necessary to make value judgments, evaluating everything that comes to us. We will have to determine if whatever comes our way is true, noble, honest, just, pure, lovely, and of good report, and act accordingly.

If Christians made those determinations, gossip, among other things, would cease instantly. Gossip is usually at least partially distorted and embellished. It is generally not something of good report, so it is certainly not good to talk about.

There will certainly be times when we have to

discuss someone. However, we must take care not to be judgmental, or to assume that because someone else said something, it is automatically true. When someone tries to tell me about someone or something, I always say, "Maybe that's not true." And many times, it really is not true. We need to be very careful because all these things will have an impact on our faith and our lives, as well as on the person who is being talked about.

Does It Have Virtue?

The latter part of Philippians 4:8 states this: ... if *there is any virtue and if there is anything praiseworthy—meditate on these things.* Virtue means "moral goodness." If there is virtue present in what you hear about something, and it is praiseworthy, and all the other things mentioned in this verse are present, then go ahead and think on what you heard, and praise God for it.

This also means there are many things one should not think about, because those things are not just, lovely, honest, or have virtue or praise about them. Satan will constantly assault our minds with such things, but the only way he knows his assaults are succeeding is when we pick up a thought and begin discussing it. The Bible says that we can just as easily dismiss that thought and concentrate instead on the Word.

Second Corinthians 10:1-5:

> *Now I, Paul, myself am pleading with you by the meekness and gentleness of Christ—who in*

presence am lowly among you, but being absent am bold toward you.

But I beg you that when I am present I may not be bold with that confidence by which I intend to be bold against some, who think of us as if we walked according to the flesh.

For though we walk in the flesh, we do not war according to the flesh.

For the weapons of our warfare are not carnal but mighty in God for pulling down strongholds, casting down arguments and every high thing that exalts itself against the knowledge of God, bringing every thought into captivity to the obedience of Christ.

The only way we can cast down arguments and every high thing that exalts itself against the knowledge of God and bring every thought into captivity to the obedience of Christ is by having an accurate knowledge of the Word. We have to measure everything by the Word, to determine whether or not it exalts itself against the knowledge of God. Whatever that thought, that concern, or that worry that pops into our minds, we have to examine it by the Word of God. If it measures up, we can think about it. If it does not, we need to get rid of it. Throw it away.

3

Fear
A Robbing Spirit

SECOND TIMOTHY 1:7:
For God has not given us a spirit of fear, but of power and of love and of a sound mind.

Every born-again person receives the Spirit of power, of love, and of a sound mind when he or she becomes born again. If you are a Christian you have that Spirit.

Notice also that in this verse Paul uses the phrase, *a spirit of fear.* Fear is a spirit. It is an agent of Satan, and that agent will steal the blessings of God from you by robbing you of your faith.

Before we go any further, we need to clarify what we mean when we use the word *fear.* Sometimes we use words that don't convey what we really mean. For instance, someone may say that he or she is afraid of fire, but if we were to analyze the situation we may find that they are not truly afraid of fire.

Personally, I don't have a fear of fire. I have fire in the engine of my automobile when I'm driving. I have had fire in my home water heaters. Fire cooks my food. But there is no way I will stick my hand into a fire, because I know that fire burns. So even though I am not afraid of fire, I do have respect for it.

The point is, we need to separate things we may be afraid of from the things for which we have a respect. Once we accomplish that, we can make the effort to deal with the things through which the spirit of fear tries to dominate us.

Here is how someone can tell when a spirit of fear is attempting to dominate them: when whatever it is they are afraid of causes them to panic or become paralyzed with fright, that is a spirit of fear in action. I have known of people who became so uncontrollable with fear when they got into an elevator that they would start to shake, choke, panic, or break into a sweat. There is no reason for anyone to be afraid of getting into an elevator.

There is also no reason for anyone to be afraid of enclosed places. There is nothing about an enclosed area that has any problem with them or any control over them. The same goes for high places. Heights should not bother people. God is high and lifted up. Heaven is high. we have a problem with high places, how are we going to go to heaven?

There are things that occur that can open the door for the spirit of fear to jump in and control us. At one point, fear had me controlled when it came to water. There I was, a grown adult male and had lived all my life in the Los Angeles area where you are never far from the ocean, and I could not put my head under the water until I was in my forties.

Why would I be afraid of water? Because something had happened to me in my childhood. I believe it had something to do with the ocean, but then my mind goes blank, and I don't remember the details. But it caused fear to come in, and for many years if I even turned my head the wrong way in the shower and got water in my nose, I would panic.

The same kind of fear gripped me when flying on airplanes. Airplanes had never done anything to me, but I was literally terrified of flying on one. I remember an incident in which my father took me up in an airplane. I can remember screaming and crying in that plane, but that's all I can recall. Apparently, there was something about that incident that caused my mind to blank out, and which allowed the spirit of fear access to me in that area.

The ironic thing was that I loved airplanes. I was a boy during World War II, and I had every picture of military aircrafts I could get my hands on. I could name every airplane America had, plus some of those that Germany, Japan and England had. I loved to work on jigsaw puzzles of airplanes. But you could not get me in an airplane to save my life.

Until I learned how to walk by faith, the spirit of fear had control over me in those two areas—water and flying. Once I learned to operate in faith, I broke that spirit, and conquered those fears.

I learned to scuba dive and have been down as far as 80 feet under the ocean. It is the same water that was there before, but I found out that I had not been given a spirit of fear and that I did not have to accept anything that God did not give me. Fear is a malevolent spirit that has no legal right to have any influence over our lives.

Many phobias that people have are actually spirits.

That doesn't mean they are possessed, such as when a demon has control over a person. It just means that they have allowed a fear spirit to come in and influence them in some particular area. Whenever they approach that area, that spirit begins to talk to them and exercise authority over them.

Some people hold onto little things. They may think, "There is no big thing about being afraid of dogs. I don't run into dogs that often." But when there is a friendly setting where a dog is present, they should take the opportunity to break that fear. This doesn't mean they should find some dog that's baring its fangs and foaming at the mouth and put their hand in its mouth. We should show some respect for things that can harm us, but we should not be afraid to walk down a street because there is a dog down there. If anything, the dog should be afraid of us. As Spirit-filled believers, we have been given the power of the Holy Spirit. We are the ones about whom the Bible says in First John 4:4:... *He who is in you is greater than he who is in the world.*

Physical Challenges, Spiritual Causes

Fear is not the only thing that can be caused by demonic spirits. We have several instances in the Bible in which something that manifested physically was caused by demonic forces. For example, in Luke 13:10-16:

> *Now He [Jesus] was teaching in one of the syna-gogues on the Sabbath.*
>
> *And behold, there was a woman who had a spirit of infirmity eighteen years, and was bent over and could in no way raise herself up.*
>
> *But when Jesus saw her, He called her to Him and said to her, "Woman, you are loosed from your infirmity."*
>
> *And He laid His hands on her, and immedi-ately she was made straight, and glorified God.*
>
> *But the ruler of the synagogue answered with indignation, because Jesus had healed on the Sabbath; and he said to the crowd, "There are six days on which men ought to work; therefore come and be healed on them, and not on the Sabbath day."*
>
> *The Lord then answered him and said, "Hypocrite! Does not each one of you on the*

Sabbath loose his ox or donkey from the stall,
and lead it away to water it?

"So ought not this woman, being a daughter
of Abraham, whom Satan has bound—think of
it—for eighteen years, be loosed from this bond
on the Sabbath?"

This woman had a spirit of infirmity which was sent to her from Satan. Many times, there is a demonic spirit enforcing a sickness or disease. In some of these situations, you'll need more than prayer or the laying on of hands to deliver that person. You need to bind and cast out that spirit before that person can be healed.

That is why we need to continually pray and covet earnestly the best gifts of the Spirit to be in operation so that those gifts can reveal to us what is needed in a given situation. These gifts do not work by themselves. We need to desire them. It is not necessarily the point of you having them or me having them, but that they function and operate when we come together as the corporate Body of Christ. That way, the needs of the body can be supernaturally ministered to in whatever those needs may be.

We have another kind of spirit mentioned in Mark 5:1-2:

Then they came to the other side of the sea, to
the country of the Gadarenes.

And when He had come out of the boat,

immediately there met Him out of the tombs a man with an unclean spirit.

Here we have an unclean spirit. There are other places in the four Gospels that talk about deaf and dumb spirits. These are entities, spirit creatures that can get into a person's life through various methods, but they need to be discerned and cast out.

We also must be careful not to get into the mindset of some that believe everything is caused by a spirit. Some things can be caused by spirits, but many times, it is just a case of the person not taking authority over his or her body, mind and actions.

Some people talk about having the spirit of gluttony. That is not a spirit, but rather a lack of self-control. Sometimes it is easier to say something is a spirit than it is to take authority over yourself. What people must realize is that they must learn to practice discipline and say no to that third slice of apple pie.

Oppression, Obsession, Possession

When a person is being influenced, say by a spirit of fear, it does not necessarily mean that the spirit is possessing that person. There are three stages of demonic presence. The first stage is oppression, which is an outward influence that everyone is subject to.

If the person does not deal with the influence, it can move to the second stage of the demonic presence, which is obsession. Obsession is when a spirit gets ahold of a person's mind. Lastly, when the obsessive spirit moves from the person's mind into his or her spirit, that is the third stage, called possession.

Some people claim that Christians cannot be possessed. That is like saying Christians cannot sin. Christians can do anything anyone else can do. They can commit the sin leading to death (the original Kings James calls it "the sin unto death") by renouncing Christ and becoming eternally lost. No, they don't have to do it, but they are able to do it if they so choose.

Christians can also let a spirit in, listen to it, and let it possess them. It does not necessarily change their relationship with God, but it will certainly affect their enjoyment of the Christian life.

However, a Spirit-filled believer cannot go to bed tonight as a Spirit-filled, victoriously living Christian, and wake up in the morning possessed by a demon. That cannot happen; otherwise, none of us would have any protection against demonic forces.

What happens is that demons work their way in over a period of time, beginning with oppression, then obsession as one begins to heed what the spirit says. Eventually, it drops down into their spirits and possesses them. However, it cannot do that without their cooperation, so there is nothing to be afraid of unless that person consciously entertains that spirit's influence.

Here is an example of what I mean about how a

person can give a spirit permission to possess them: there was a lady who wanted to be very spiritual. She would go to various meetings, and would hear other people's testimonies about how the Lord had spoken to them or appeared to them in a vision. She became fixated with wanting God to talk to her, and this fixation became an obsession.

Finally, some entity spoke to the woman supernaturally, and she thought it was God. Her loved ones recognized that she had been deceived and tried to get her some much-needed help. They took her to meeting after meeting, yet the entity still operated in her. Finally, they took her to a Kenneth E. Hagin crusade. As Hagin, the prophet, was getting ready to minister, he learned by the word of knowledge what the woman's problem was, and was instructed by the Holy Spirit on how to proceed. He did not minister to her in public. Instead, he waited until the service was over and talked to her privately.

By the Spirit, Hagin told her all the things I have just mentioned. Then, he said, "Now, sister, I can help you. I can take authority over this thing and cast it out, if you want it to be cast out." But the woman said, "I don't want it to be cast out. I want to hear this voice." Hagin told her, "In that case, there is nothing I can do for you."

If that woman wanted the spirit, there was nothing anyone could do about it. She had to have a desire to be delivered, but she wanted to hear that voice. It was supernatural, but it was the wrong voice. It had her permission to operate in her life.

A lot has to happen for an evil spirit to get control of a person. However, a spirit can get into your soul, and into your body, like the spirit of infirmity in the woman we read about in the thirteenth chapter of Luke. The unclean spirit found in the fifth chapter of Mark's Gospel had control of a man's soul. It governed his body so that he acted in ways that were unclean. So demons can operate in your spirit, soul, or body, if you allow them.

When a person accepts Jesus as his personal Savior and Lord, evil spirits are automatically driven from the believer's recreated spirit. However, it is up to the believer to take authority over any demonic spirits in his or her body. We must cast out any spirit not of God, and believe it is gone.

Once the spirit has been cast out, don't tolerate the actions that spirit would try to enforce upon your life. Stay away from areas where that spirit will work on you. Avoid circumstances, people, or places that would give that spirit re-entry into your life. For instance, if you always lose your paycheck when you go to the racetrack, don't go to the racetrack, don't talk to any bookies, and don't buy a racing form. That way, you will not lose any money at the racetrack.

How Fear Will Rob Us

We are protected from demonic powers such as the spirit of fear, but we must use our faith and the Word to maintain that freedom. This is where fighting "the good fight" comes in.

The enemy is always trying to steal your faith, or at least render it ineffective. But we have a choice as to whether we accept its presence in our lives. That is what makes the good fight of faith good. You don't have to accept any of the things the devil may throw your way because you can defeat them with God's Word.

We have a classic example of how fear works against our faith in Matthew 14:22-31, in the story of Jesus walking on the water.

> *Immediately Jesus made His disciples get into the boat and go before Him to the other side, while He sent the multitude away.*
>
> *And when He had sent the multitude away, He went up on the mountain by Himself to pray. Now when evening came, He was alone there.*
>
> *But the boat was now in the middle of the sea, tossed by the waves, for the wind was contrary.*
>
> *Now in the fourth watch of the night Jesus went to them, walking on the sea.*
>
> *And when the disciples saw Him walking on the sea, they were troubled saying, "It is a ghost!" And they cried out for fear.*
>
> *But immediately Jesus spoke to them, saying, "Be of good cheer! It is I; do not be afraid."*
>
> *And Peter answered Him and said, "Lord, if it is You, command me to come to You on the water."*

> So He said, "Come." And when Peter had come
> down out of the boat, he walked on the water to
> go to Jesus.
>
> But when he saw that the wind was boisterous,
> he was afraid; and beginning to sink he cried out,
> saying,
>
> "Lord, save me!"
>
> And immediately Jesus stretched out His hand
> and caught him, and said to him, "O you of little
> faith, why did you doubt?"

Peter doubted because he began to fear. When fear came, faith left. That was why Jesus said, *"O you of little faith."* If Peter had had great faith, he would have walked back with Jesus to the boat without thinking about it.

When Jesus told Peter, "Come," that implied two things. It implied that Peter had God's permission to defy the laws of nature, and that he had the ability to do so. Not only that, but it says in the same verse, *And when Peter had come down out of the boat, he walked on the water to go to Jesus.* Peter walked on the water! He actually did it! But he then made the mistake of taking his eyes off Jesus and looking at the wind and the waves. Once he did that, he allowed fear to come in, which robbed Peter of completing a wonderful miracle.

Power, Love, and a Sound Mind

We read in 2 Timothy 1:7, *For God has not given us a spirit of fear, but of power and of love and of a sound mind.* Power, love, and a sound mind are all wrapped up in one spirit—the Holy Spirit, the third person of the Godhead.

> *For God has not given us a spirit of fear, but of power and of love and of a sound mind.*

The word *power* in this instance is the Greek word *dunamis,* which means "divine ability." We need that divine or supernatural ability because we are dealing with a supernatural enemy, Satan. There is no way a natural individual can have any success battling the supernatural entity, so God has provided assistance for us. The Greek word for the Holy Spirit is the word *paraclete,* or *parakletos,* and it means "an assistant."

Imagine that you are attempting to pick up something that is too heavy for you. Someone kneels beside you, and together, the two of you pick it up. That is how the Holy Spirit works when He assists us. Anyone who says he doesn't need the Holy Spirit either doesn't know what he is talking about, or either he likes to work very hard at going nowhere.

...and of love...

You need to have the Spirit of God energize your faith so you can love people. You cannot love humankind with God-kind of love without the God-kind of power, because people are not always lovable. They can be ornery, undependable, critical, full of strife, mean, and up one minute and down the next. You cannot always depend on them, and you will need supernatural help to love them with a mature, God kind of love.

...and of a sound mind...

A sound mind does not simply refer to those who are not in a mental ward. It refers to those whose minds are fixed on the Word of the living God. Our minds are not sound if we base our lives on anything other than God's plainly revealed Word.

Once we fix our minds on the Word to the point where they are sound, the Spirit of God energizes our minds, and gives them the capability to operate in supernatural dimensions. Otherwise, our minds will continue to operate in natural dimensions, and be limited in their operation. That is because the natural world is a limited world. The supernatural realm, or spirit realm by contrast, has no limits. That is one reason why Paul says in Romans 12:1-2:

> *I beseech you therefore, brethren, by the mercies of God, that you present your bodies a living sacrifice, holy, acceptable to God, which is your reasonable service.*
>
> *And do not be conformed to this world, but be transformed by the renewing of your mind, that you may prove what is that good and acceptable and perfect will of God.*

Paul says that it is our responsibility to present our bodies as a living sacrifice. However, we cannot do that naturally, simply because we cannot do what God tells us to do solely by natural processes. We need supernatural help to transcend being conformed to this world, and to transform ourselves by the renewing of our minds.

The reason we cannot do it on our own is because the physical world is the only world we have ever known. We have learned everything we know here, and we are so conditioned to it that it is impossible to transcend it and move into the realm of the Spirit on our own. The Holy Spirit is the link, so to speak, between the natural and the supernatural.

The way we release the power of the Holy Spirit to help us is by speaking with tongues. That is why the devil fights the idea of speaking with tongues so much and creates so much confusion about the subject. He knows that once people start speaking with tongues, they will be in position to blow him away. He doesn't want that, so he tries to scare people away from it with confusion, deception, and fear.

Living to the Master Plan

For God has not given us a spirit of fear, but of power and of love and of a sound mind.

A *sound mind* is a mind that is settled in the Word and directs the body in line with the revealed Word of

God. That is the master plan. No contractor will erect a building without a master plan, yet Christians are attempting to build their lives every day without a plan. That is why many of them end up in divorce court. If they don't end up in divorce court, they stay together but are miserable. They suffer, the children suffer, and the children's attitude on marriage sours because of what they see in their homes.

We cannot build our lives solely on the words "I love the Lord." Our loving the Lord is good, and we should love Him, but loving the Lord will not do anything to improve our lifestyle. We need the plan. If we didn't need it, why would God have wasted time having the Bible written, translated, and printed? God's Word is the plan for our lives, and we need the Holy Spirit to help us read the blueprints.

We had a room addition put on our house several years ago. During the time the room was under construction, the contractor was telling me about a certain thing they were going to do using something called "glulam." He kept saying, "glulam," and I thought, "What in the world is he talking about? Is he going to glue a lamb?" He even had it on the blueprint, and I still didn't know what it was.

Finally, I asked the contractor what a *glulam* was, and he told me it was one of the strongest things you could ever make. A glulam is lots of pieces of wood overlapped and glued (laminated) together. When all those pieces are laminated, you have more strength than you would have with a plain, straight piece of wood. The gluelam the contractor was planning to use was a big beam that would go across the main part of the addition. It would help support the second story, and also give strength to the lower story. The gluelam would work the same as the backbone works inside the body. Our backbone supports our bodies because our ribs, shoulders, legs, and head are all connected to it. Remove the backbone, and our bodies collapse.

We need the Holy Spirit to find out where the gluelam is in the Christian's life, so we can know what to do. People try to build their lives without the Word. They attend churches where the Word is not taught, and they receive nothing. That is why their lives are so shattered. It doesn't mean they don't love God, or that they aren't genuinely Christians, but it does mean that most aren't successful in life. They are defeated, scared, and dominated by the world system.

Don't let the spirit of fear—or anything else the devil throws at you—have place in your life. Take charge over it and take advantage of the supernatural help God has given you. Thank God we have the Spirit of power, of love, and of a sound mind. Stand on that. Do not give the devil any place. Learn your covenant rights, stand on them, and you cannot lose. You can only win.

4

The Battle
for the Mind

SECOND CORINTHIANS 10:1-5:

Now I, Paul, myself am pleading with you by the meekness and gentleness of Christ—who in presence am lowly among you, but being absent am bold toward you.

But I beg you that when I am present I may not be bold with that confidence by which I intend to be bold against some, who think of us as if we walked according to the flesh.

For though we walk in the flesh, we do not war according to the flesh.

For the weapons of our warfare are not carnal but mighty in God for pulling down strongholds,

casting down arguments and every high thing that exalts itself against the knowledge of God, bringing every thought into captivity to the obedience of Christ.

When Satan and his forces come at you with worry, fear, unforgiveness, or any other kind of negative thought, the place they will assault you is in your mind. Of course, the devil will move from our minds to our bodies, but his first area of attack is mental. That is why Paul writes in verses three and four:

> *For though we walk in the flesh, we do not war according to the flesh.*
> *For the weapons of our warfare are not carnal but mighty in God for pulling down strongholds.*

The mind is the arena or battleground of faith. That is where the battle for your faith will be won or lost, depending on how well you have prepared yourself for battle by developing a sound mind.

At this point, let me make something very clear. I'm not referring to anything that has to do with Science of Mind as a religion, or anything having to do with Science of Living or Christian Science. What I'm saying is entirely different from what those organizations teach. We are discussing what is written in the Word of God. Much of what I refer to may be used by those sects, but that doesn't mean that what I'm referring to is from those sources.

For the Spirit-filled, Spirit-led, Spirit-guided Christian, who has developed a sound mind and knows how to rightly divide the Word of Truth, the center of his motivation should be his spirit. His spirit should control his mind, and his mind should control his body.

Too many Christians don't renew their minds, and by that don't let their spirits control them. Satan gets into their mind realm, scrambles it, and causes them to act in ways that bring reproaches to Christ. That unrenewed mind also keeps them in sickness, disease, poverty, fear, and defeat, to name just a few things. That is why Paul warns us in Romans 8:6:

> *For to be carnally minded is death, but to be spiritually minded is life and peace.*

That is also why he tells us in Second Corinthians 10:5:...*casting down arguments and every high thing....* It's interesting that he uses the words *high thing.* There are many things which appear lofty and idealistic yet are not inspired of God and may actually be an abomination in His sight. They are traps, and if we aren't careful, we can get sucked into one of them.

Paul continues in verse five with:...*bringing every thought into captivity to the obedience of Christ.* We are to be the custodians of our thought life. If God wanted to control our thinking, He would have made us robots, and programmed us from the beginning. However, He gave us the ability to make choices, decisions, and value judgments. He gave us what is called "free will."

All God wants to do is show us the way we can

control ourselves, so we can have the greatest degree of benefit. Always remember that God doesn't need us to be God. We need Him to be who and what we are. Anything He strives to get us to do is not for *His* benefit, but for *our* benefit, so we can be blessed and can be what we should be.

Minds Blinded by Satan

Satan blinds the minds and thoughts of people in many areas. There is no reason to kill someone. We did not give any person life, so why would we take his or her life from them? Why would a man kill his wife and children, then sit down and wait in the living room while the police break in, and tell them, "Something just came over me. I don't understand it"? His wife and kids are dead, he has a smoking gun in his hand, and he says he doesn't know why he did it.

Why does a man hold up a bank? That in itself wouldn't be so bad, but the poor fool is endangering his own life. He could get shot while trying to flee the scene. It's ridiculous, illogical and irrational, but people do nonsensical things. The same is true of drug abuse. In spite of all the people who have gone down the tubes overdosing, many drug-abusers still take a chance, and think, "It won't happen to me."

We have to guard our minds. No one's mind is off limits to the influence of the devil. You are living in a fool's paradise if you think you are immune to Satan's trickery. You don't have to yield to the trickery, but you need to know that Satan can influence your mind.

Your mind is open to both God and to the devil. You are the one who decides which way to go. You can gravitate toward the devil, or you can gravitate toward God—you are the one in control.

Second Corinthians 4:1-4:

> *Therefore, since we have this ministry, as we have received mercy, we do not lose heart.*
>
> *But we have renounced the hidden things of shame, not walking in craftiness nor handling the word of God deceitfully, but by manifestation of the truth commending ourselves to every man's conscience in the sight of God.*
>
> *But even if our gospel is veiled [or hidden], it is veiled to those who are perishing,*
>
> *Whose minds the god of this age has blinded, who do not believe, lest the light of the gospel of the glory of Christ, who is the image of God, should shine on them.*

Notice who is blinding the minds. Paul says,... *the god of this age* (or as the original King James Bible translates it, "the god of this world"). Not God the Creator, but the god of this world.

Whether you know it or not, this world is under the domination of Satan. He is real. He wants you to think that he is not real, so he can keep pulling the wool over your eyes and get you to blame God for what he does. But he is real, and he is out there. Let me show you a revelation that proves my point.

Here is God Almighty, who says in John 3:16, *"For God so loved the world that He gave his only begotten Son, that whoever believes in Him should not perish but have everlasting life."* He sends the Light—His Son Jesus Christ—so people can find salvation. But Satan wants us to believe that He also blinds our eyes so we cannot believe that which He has given us to believe. Of course, that makes no sense whatsoever.

It must therefore mean that one force is doing the blinding, and another force doing the opening of the eyes. The God of all ages is the one who loves us and gave His Son for us. Satan, who is a counterfeit god, is trying to gain people's allegiance and attention. He is the one who blinds people's eyes so they cannot see the glorious light of the gospel, and will go down the tubes with him.

That is the reason we need the Word of God. It is the Word that is the light, that takes away the darkness so we can see.

Tested the Same Way Christ Was

As I said before, none of us are outside the realm of satanic encroachment on our thinking. That includes Jesus Christ, who *was in all points tempted as we are* (Hebrews 4:15). He was tried and tested by the same devil who is trying and testing you and me. Satan attacked Jesus in the same way he attacks us—in the mind.

Matthew 4:1-3:

> *Then Jesus was led up by the Spirit into the wilderness to be tempted by the devil.*
> *And when He had fasted forty days and forty nights, afterward He was hungry.*
> *Now when the tempter came to Him, he said, "If You are the Son of God, command that these stones become bread."*

Satan's attack is to always cast doubt on the truthfulness of God's Word. He will always question us concerning what God says in an attempt to get us to compromise the Word. That is how Satan tricked Adam and Eve in the Garden of Eden. God specifically stated, *"You shall not eat...."* and the devil inquired, *"Has God indeed said...?"* Did God really say that? The minute you ask, "Did God say that or not," you are messing up, and you will lose the game.

Satan tried using the same tactic on Jesus. In Matthew 4:3, Satan said, *"If You are the Son of God...?"* The devil knew who Jesus was, but he wanted Jesus to ask Himself, "I wonder if I am the Son of God?" Matthew 4:4 shows us how Jesus handled the situation, and how we should handle the tempter when he comes to us:

But He answered and said, "It is written, 'Man shall not live by bread alone, but by every word that proceeds from the mouth of God.'"

Jesus did not fool around saying, "Hey, devil, don't you know I am the Son of God? Here is my I.D. and my Social Security card." He just said, "It is written," and that was the end of the discussion on that subject.

That was not the end of the devil tempting Jesus, however. He changed the subject and came at Jesus twice more, still trying to get Jesus to question God's Word. But every time, Jesus told the devil, "It is written," and the devil finally gave up.

That is what we must do.

When Satan shoots thoughts into your mind, you cannot let yourself entertain them. If you do, the devil will wipe you out. Paul says, *casting down arguments and every high thing that exalts itself against the knowledge of God, bringing every thought into captivity.* That means you must capture those thoughts and not let them run wild.

There is not a day that passes in which the devil does not try to put something on me. There have been times when my body has said to me, "Fred, will you please quit fighting? Just get some medication, and let the doctors put you out for a week, so you can lie down and relax." Satan knows enough about human nature to realize that ordinarily, if you keep hitting someone, that person will finally throw in the towel and give up.

I know too much of the Word to do that, so I cast down that argument, and bring that high thought into line with the Word of God If that argument doesn't fit the Word, I don't accept it; I cast it down. The Word says that if I serve Him, He will take sickness away from the midst of me (Exodus 23:25), so there is no point in me being sick. And as Paul reminds us in Second Corinthians 5:7, *For we walk by faith, not by sight.* That is part of our assignment—to walk by what the Word says, not by what we feel. We must let the Word be our governing force, not our experiences. Isaiah 26:3 tells us:

> *You will keep him in perfect peace, Whose mind*
> *is stayed on You, Because he trusts in You.*

How do we keep our mind on God? By keeping our minds on the Word. It is the Word of God that brings information and revelation about the knowledge of God; and when we have the knowledge of God, we can be at peace. We know that our bills are paid, every need is met, our bodies are healed, and our families are well, because we know God is backing us up every step of the way.

5

Losing Hope

EVEN WHEN WE guard against the negative thoughts the devil throws at us, we can still be defeated in living the God-kind of life. In fact, it is very easy to do so. If our faith is not up to the level of our hopes, our faith will not bring those hopes into manifestation. When we lose hope, for all intents and purposes, we also shut down our faith.

You may think it doesn't matter what you hope, because the Bible says to *walk by faith, not by sight.* And that is true: We should make it a point to walk by faith. But the Bible also tells us in Hebrews 10:23, *Let us hold fast the confession of our hope without wavering, for He who promised is faithful.* The word *hope* may seem inappropriate, but in truth it is exceedingly important.

Before I learned to walk by faith, all my wife and I lived on was hope. Hope did not do anything to change our circumstances, just as it will not change what happens in your life. Faith is what releases the power of God to change your life; hope will simply keep you alive until things change.

However, to truly walk by faith, you must have hope. Paul writes in Hebrews 11:1, *Now faith is the substance of things hoped for....* Hope sets the goal, and faith obtains the goal for us. Hope and faith must work together.

Everyone should have a goal. If you never set a goal, guess what? You will never attain one. That is why many people—and, sad to say, many Christians—never achieve anything. They never set any specific goals, so they have nothing for their faith to obtain.

I want to challenge you readers to set goals for you and your faith to strive toward. I don't know about you, but I have reached at least most of the goals I have set for myself. Some of those objectives have not yet manifested; and sometimes, things take more than twelve months to manifest. The point is, as I have just stated, if you do not set goals, you will likely never reach any.

When you set your goals, make sure you don't set them so high that you become frustrated and give up without doing anything. The devil would love to see you to do exactly that. He would love to see you set a goal too big for yourself, then give up, saying, "That faith business does not work!" It would make his job considerably easier.

When you first start setting goals, it would probably be better to set short-term goals, rather than long-term ones. You may need to take a hop, a skip and a jump to reach a long-term goal, but it will be well worth your efforts in the end.

Stay Steadfast

When Paul tells us in Hebrews 10:23 to *hold fast the confession of our hope,* he means for us to hold tight, to grab ahold and not to let go. Or as he puts it in First Corinthians 15:58:

> *Therefore, my beloved brethren, be steadfast....*

Steadfast means "to remain constant." Too many Christians are spasmodic. They are in the first row of the church one month, the fourth row the next month, the ninth row the month after that, and after a while you cannot find them in the church at all!

You must determine that you are going to stick to your goals "come hell or high water." It means if hell rises against you, if the water rises and the tide comes in—whatever happens, you will stay with it. That takes discipline and commitment. Sometimes it will take considerable work to keep that commitment on the same level at which you started. But if you are at all serious about obtaining your goal, you must do it.

> *Therefore, my beloved brethren, be steadfast, immovable....*

Again, too many Christians are movable. They are moved by every little wind that comes up. But notice what happens when you do not move, but "stay on course."

...always abounding in the work of the Lord, knowing that your labor is not in vain in the Lord.

In other words, whatever it is that you desire will come to pass if you stay with it. In the midst of being steadfast, you will come up against persecutions. In Revelation 3:15-16, Jesus makes this statement:

> *"I know your works, that you are neither cold nor hot. I could wish you were cold or hot.*
>
> *"So then, because you are lukewarm, and neither cold nor hot, I will vomit you out of My mouth."*

Jesus does not like you lukewarm, and Satan doesn't like you hot. Satan will throw everything that he can against you to hinder you from reaching your goals. Don't always assume that because bad things come against you, that you have done something wrong. It may be that you are doing something right! For that reason, you must examine each individual situation when it occurs. Keep in mind what Jesus said in John 15:18-19:

> *"If the world hates you, you know that it hated Me before it hated you.*
>
> *"If you were of the world, the world would love its own. Yet because you are not of the world, but I chose you out of the world, therefore the world hates you."*

When Jesus refers to the world, He's talking about Satan, because Satan is the god of this world. He is not the god of us Christians, nor is he the god of the universe, but he is the god of this world. So the world's systems put pressure on you, and laugh because you say you are a Christian. All that is designed to make you either lukewarm or cold.

You can handle the pressure. Jesus did, so you are running in good company. Jesus said, *"If they persecuted Me, they will also persecute you"* (John 15:20). They called Him everything but a child of God. Persecution is part of the warfare, and it will come, but like Jesus, you can win. As Paul phrases it in Second Corinthians 4:8-9:

> *We are hard-pressed on every side, yet not crushed; we are perplexed, but not in despair;*
> *Persecuted, but not forsaken; struck down, but not destroyed....*

The word *perplexed* in verse eight means "to be at loss mentally." Situations arise, and in the natural and you cannot figure out what to do. But when you are walking in the Word, walking by faith and by the Spirit, you have inside information—information inside the Word of God, which is outside the realm of human reason. Your mind may fail you, but the Spirit of God has all the answers. When you turn to Him, He will guide you right out of the situation.

Paul writes in 2 Timothy 3:10-11:

> *But you have carefully followed my doctrine, manner of life, purpose, faith, longsuffering, love perseverance,*
> *Persecution, affliction, which happened to me at Antioch, at Iconium, at Lystra—what persecutions I endured. And out of them all the Lord delivered me*

Do you think God loved Paul more than He loves you? I tell you no! Jesus said in John 3:16, *"For God so loved the world that He gave His only begotten Son...."* If Jesus said that he and the Father loved Paul more than the rest of us, we would be in trouble. But God loves us all on an equal basis. He doesn't have any favorite kids. It may seem at times that He does, but that is only because some kids are more obedient. That is why they get the benefits. The ones who are not quite as obedient don't get all the benefits.

If you walk by God's Word, He will do the same for you as He did for Paul. He delivered Paul, so He will deliver you—provided you endure as Paul did.

Paul adds in 2 Timothy 3:12:

> *Yes, and all who desire to live godly in Christ Jesus will suffer persecution.*

The word *suffer* has a different meaning here than it usually does in English. Here, it means "to put up with."

What Paul is saying in this verse is that everyone who will live godly in Christ Jesus will have to put up with persecution.

There are only two ways to avoid persecution. One is to get rid of the devil, which we cannot do. The other way is to not read the Bible, not pray, not tithe, not speak in tongues, and not operate in the realm of the Spirit. In other words, if nobody knows you are a Christian, you won't have persecution because the devil will not bother you.

Why should Satan waste any ammunition on you if you are no threat to his kingdom? The people who say, "Praise the Lord! I believe I receive! This is the victory that overcomes the world, even my faith!" are the ones he shoots at, because they are a threat to his kingdom.

To repeat what I said before, deliverance is at hand— if we are steadfast and stand fast through persecution. We read that in Second Timothy 3:11, and Paul reaffirms it in Second Timothy 4:18, where he says:

> *And the Lord will deliver me from every evil work and preserve me for His heavenly kingdom. To Him be the glory forever and ever. Amen!*

If we are delivered from every evil work, then none of those works can get through to us, and we should not be overcome by any of them.

Using Faith with Hope

In Second Corinthians 4:17-18, Paul makes another important statement about persecution, and he adds something
else that is very important. He starts out by saying:

> *For our light affliction, which is but for a
> moment....*

Isn't that something? Paul had been shipwrecked,
stoned, thrown in prison and persecuted, and after
everything he had gone through, he said, *For our light
affliction.* Hooray, Paul!

> *For our light affliction, which is but for a moment,
> is working for us a far more exceeding and eternal
> weight of glory, while we do not look at the things
> which are seen, but at the things which are not
> seen. For the things which are seen are temporary,
> but the things which are not seen are eternal.*

How do you look at things that are not seen? With
the eye of faith. Hebrews 11:1 tells us, *Now faith is the
substance of things hoped for, the evidence of things
not seen.* If we allow the things we see to determine
where we are, we will be sidetracked from our goal. But
if we allow our faith, our hope, and what God's Word
says to determine the path we walk, and faint not, we
will see our goal met in due season.

However, let me caution you about one thing, because

some people, when they attempt to walk by faith, go off the deep end, and get things confused and mixed up.

Paul is *not* saying that the things which are seen don't exist. He is simply telling us not to look at them. Many people, when they think they are walking by faith, go around saying, "sickness is not there," or "poverty is not there." That is not what Paul is telling us to do. If the things which are seen were not real, how could you see them? You cannot see something that does not exist.

When Paul says, *while we look not at the things which are seen,* he is simply telling us that the things which are seen should not be the things we use as guidelines by which to walk. We should not deny that they are there. If you are having a heart attack, don't try to con yourself by saying, "I'm not having a heart attack." Put your faith on the line for being healed of it and call the doctor. Saying that malady is not there will make you only one thing—DEAD.

You also need to understand this: Though you walk by faith, your faith will be tried and tested. It may look at times as if everything is coming unglued at once, but all that is designed to try, test or destroy your faith because that is what the devil is out to do. Don't think you will walk through on a flowery bed of ease. It is easy from the standpoint that you know you will win, but you will have to put forth the physical exertion necessary to manifest that victory in your life.

While you are putting forth that effort, one scripture that will help you considerably is James 1:2-3:

My brethren, count it all joy when you fall into various trials....

James did not say it was joy, and it is definitely not joy when the pressure is on. But he tells us to count it *as* joy. Treat it as joy. In other words, have the attitude that it is joy. If you do that, you will never be defeated.

My brethren, count it all joy when you fall into various trials,
    knowing that the testing of your faith produces patience.

Patience means "endurance." The trying or testing or proving of your faith will build up your spiritual endurance. How do you build up endurance to run further? Keep on running and increase the distance little by little over a period of time. Faith works the same way. The trying of your faith will build up your spiritual endurance, and you will be able to stand. You will need that enduring kind of faith to stand against everything the devil throws at you.

First Peter 1:3-5:

Blessed be the God and Father of our Lord Jesus Christ, who according to His abundant mercy has

begotten us again to a living hope through the res-
urrection of Jesus Christ from the dead,
   to an inheritance incorruptible and undefiled
and that does not fade away, reserved in heaven
for you,
   who are kept by the power of God through
faith for salvation ready to be revealed in the
last time.

How are we kept by the power of God? Through faith.
First Peter 1:6-9:

In this you greatly rejoice, though now for a little
while, if need be, you have been grieved by var-
ious trials,
   that the genuineness of your faith, being much
more precious than gold that perishes, though it is
tested by fire, may be found to praise, honor, and
glory at revelation of Jesus Christ.
   whom having not seen you love. Though now
you do not see Him, yet believing, you rejoice
with joy inexpressible and full of glory,
   receiving the end of your faith—the salvation
of your souls.

Our faith is tried, or literally proved, but it is more
precious than gold in the sight of God. Actually, it will
be more precious to you once it has been tried, because
it is only faith that has been tried that you know you
can rely on. If you have never used your faith, you

cannot really be sure of it. Once you have faith to go through everything the devil can throw at you, and you have come out on top, you have no fear or intimidation when you go into any kind of new venture, because you already have victories behind you.

An Example and a Stumbling Block

In the sixth chapter of Hebrews, we have one outstanding example of what will happen when we endure everything the enemy throws at us. It also shows us how many people don't reach their goals once they set them.

Hebrews 6:10-11:

> *For God is not unjust to forget your work and labor of love which you have shown toward His name, in that you have ministered to the saints, and do minister.*
>
> *And we desire that each one of you show the same diligence to the full assurance of hope until the end.*

That is, to the end of reaching your goal.

Hebrews 6:12:

> *that you do not become sluggish....*

That means shiftless and lazy, which some Christians have definitely become in terms of using their faith. As I said before, you must be steadfast. You must be constant. The only way you will reach your goals is if you do what the next few verses tell us.

Hebrews 6:12-15:

> *that you do not become sluggish, but imitate those who through faith and patience inherit the promises.*
>
> *For when God made a promise to Abraham, because He could swear by no one greater, He swore by Himself,*
>
> *saying, "Surely blessing I will bless you, and multiplying I will multiply you."*
>
> *And so, after he had patiently endured, he obtained the promise.*

Abraham is our example of how we should strive to achieve our hopes. Abraham was faithful. In fact, the original King James Bible calls him "faithful Abraham" (Galatians 3:9); he had patiently endured for years. Because he endured, was steadfast, and didn't give up, he received the son God promised him.

God has given us His promises, and if He kept His Word to Abraham, He will certainly do so with us. However, the only way we will receive what God promises is through faith and patience.

Philippians 3:13-14:

> *Brethren, I do not count myself to have apprehended* [or attained]; *but one thing I do, forgetting*

those things which are behind and reaching for-
ward to those things which are ahead,
    I press toward the goal for the prize of the
upward call of God in Christ Jesus.

The upward call of God is the abundant life in Jesus; that life is victorious in every situation and circumstance. I like the song that Johnson Oatman Jr. wrote around 1898:

I'm pressing on the upward way,
new heights I'm gaining every day.
Still praying as I onward bound,
Lord plant my feet on higher ground.
Lord lift me up and let me stand,
    by faith on heaven's table land,
    a higher plane than I have found,
Lord plant my feet on higher ground.

If you don't set goals to plant your feet on higher ground, guess what? You will never reach higher ground. You will never receive what you are hoping for.

Take heart, take courage, and take these words I have given you as exhortation. Set some goals, put your faith on the line, and go for it! Go for it in the name of Jesus!

Apostle Frederick K.C. Price

Biography

Apostle Frederick K.C. Price is the founder of Crenshaw Christian Center (CCC) in Los Angeles, California. He began CCC in 1973 and shepherded it through 35 years into a ministry of world renown, with services held since 1989 in the world-famous FaithDome.

In 1978, Apostle Price received instruction from God to begin a television broadcast. As a result, *Ever Increasing Faith Ministries* (EIFM) was launched, appearing initially in five of the nation's big-city television markets. Since that time, the broadcast has become global, and EIFM can be viewed on 58 stations in all 50 states and in 12 foreign countries. The broadcast is also heard on 15 radio programs and 19 Internet broadcast stations. Additionally, it can be viewed on the *Ever Increasing Faith* website, YouTube, Vimeo, Christian. tv and an extensive number of social media platforms.

In 1990, Apostle Price founded the Fellowship of Inner-City Word of Faith Ministries (FICWFM), which later became the Fellowship of International Christian Word of Faith Ministries before discontinuing. And in 2001, he established an East Coast church—Crenshaw Christian Center East.

A visionary and widely respected teacher, he is the

author of some 50 books on faith, healing, prosperity, the Holy Spirit and other subjects. His book, *How Faith Works,* is a recognized classic on the operation of faith and its life-changing principles. He has also authored three historic volumes under the title of *Race, Religion & Racism.* Apostle Price has sold more than 2.5 million books since 1976. His most recent works include, *The Mind: The Arena of Faith, Prosperity: Good News for God's People* and *Answered Prayer Guaranteed: The Power of Praying with Faith.*

Although Apostle Price had already begun operating under the mantle of apostle, in 2008 he was publicly affirmed as an apostle of faith. Under his gift as teacher, he established several schools for ministry and formal education on the grounds of CCC. Among them are Frederick K.C. Price III Christian Schools (preschool to 12th grade) and the Apostle Price Ministry Training Institute. Over the years, Apostle Price has received many prestigious awards—most notably, the Horatio Alger Award from the Horatio Alger Association of Distinguished Americans and the Southern Christian Leadership Council's Kelly Miller Smith Interfaith Award, both in 1998.

Apostle Price holds an honorary doctorate of divinity from Oral Roberts University in Tulsa, Oklahoma, and an honorary diploma from Rhema Bible Training Center in Broken Arrow, Oklahoma.

A year after his affirmation as apostle, and after more than 35 years as pastor, Apostle Price stepped aside to formally install his son, Frederick K. Price Jr., as pastor. He is currently the presiding prelate of CCC West and East, and serves at the helm as the chairman of CCC's board of directors. Apostle Price not only ministers in the FaithDome, but travels extensively, mostly in the United States, teaching the uncompromising Word of God.

A devoted husband and father, Apostle Price has been married to Dr. Betty R. Price for more than 65 years. They are the proud parents of four children, and have 10 grandchildren, and five great-grandchildren.

Books by Apostle Price

HOW FAITH WORKS

RACE, RELIGION & RACISM, VOLUME 1
A Bold Encounter With Division in the Church

RACE, RELIGION & RACISM, VOLUME 2
Perverting the Gospel to Subjugate a People

RACE, RELIGION & RACISM, VOLUME 3
Jesus, Christianity and Islam

HOW TO OBTAIN STRONG FAITH
Six Principles

THE HOLY SPIRIT
The Helper We All Need

THE MIND
The Arena of Faith

INTEGRITY
The Guarantee for Success

PROSPERITY
Good News for God's People

LIVING IN HOSTILE TERRITORY
A Survival Guide for the Overcoming Christian

ANSWERED PRAYER GUARANTEED

FAITH, FOOLISHNESS, OR PRESUMPTION?

IDENTIFIED WITH CHRIST:
A Complete Cycle from Defeat to Victory

THE CHRISTIAN FAMILY
Practical Insight for Family Living

DR. PRICE'S GOLDEN NUGGETS
A Treasury of Wisdom for Both Ministers and Laypeople

FIVE LITTLE FOXES OF FAITH

THE CHASTENING OF THE LORD

TESTING THE SPIRITS

BEWARE! THE LIES OF SATAN

*THE WAY, THE WALK, AND THE
WARFARE OF THE BELIEVER*
A Verse-by-Verse Study on the Book of Ephesians

THREE KEYS TO POSITIVE CONFESSION

THE PROMISED LAND
A New Era for the Body of Christ

A NEW LAW FOR A NEW PEOPLE

THE VICTORIOUS, OVERCOMING LIFE
A Verse-by-Verse Study on the Book of Colossians

PRACTICAL SUGGESTIONS FOR SUCCESSFUL MINISTRY

LIVING IN THE REALM OF THE SPIRIT

THE HOLY SPIRIT
The Missing Ingredient

IS HEALING FOR ALL?

Minibooks

THE TRUTH ABOUT... THE BIBLE

THE TRUTH ABOUT... DEATH

THE TRUTH ABOUT... DISASTERS

THE TRUTH ABOUT... FATE

THE TRUTH ABOUT ... FEAR

THE TRUTH ABOUT... HOMOSEXUALITY

THE TRUTH ABOUT... RACE

THE TRUTH ABOUT... WORRY

THE TRUTH ABOUT... GIVING

NOW FAITH IS

HOW TO BELIEVE GOD FOR A MATE

THANK GOD FOR EVERYTHING?

CONCERNING THOSE WHO HAVE FALLEN ASLEEP

THE ORIGIN OF SATAN

Specialty-size Books

WALKING IN GOD'S WORD
Through His Promises

WORDS OF WISDOM: WOW!

BUILDING ON A FIRM FOUNDATION

HOMOSEXUALITY:
State of Birth or State of Mind?

Spanish Language Books

COMO CREER EN DIOS PARA ENCONTRAR TU PAREJA

EDIFICANDONOS SOBRE UNA BASE FIRME
Una guia para el Desarrollo de Su Cristiana

To receive Apostle Price's book and discs, or to be placed on the EIF mailing list, please call:

(800) 927-3436

For more information, please write to:

Crenshaw Christian Center
P.O. Box 90000
Los Angeles, CA 90009

Or check your local TV and Internet for:

Ever Increasing Faith Ministries

or visit our website:

www.faithdome.org